Classic

AFRICAN

Authentic recipes from one of the oldest cuisines

ROSAMUND GRANT

SMITHMARK

© 1997 Anness Publishing Limited

This edition published in 1997 by
SMITHMARK Publishers, a division of US Media Holdings, Inc.
16 East 32nd Street
New York, New York 10016

SMITHMARK books are available for bulk purchase for sales promotion and for premium use. For details write or call
the manager of special sales, SMITHMARK Publishers, 16 East 32nd Street, New York, New York 10016; (212) 532-6600.

Produced by Anness Publishing Limited
Hermes House
88-89 Blackfriars Road
London SE1 8HA

ISBN 0 7651 9568 2

Publisher: Joanna Lorenz
Senior Food Editor: Linda Fraser
Project Editor: Zoe Antoniou
Designer: Ian Sandom
Illustrations: Madeleine David
Photography and styling: Patrick McLeavey
Food for photography: Annie Nichols
Jacket photography: Thomas Odulate
Lobster Piri Piri recipe supplied by Donu

Printed and bound in Singapore

Picture on frontispiece: Lamb Tagine (top), and Spiced Fried
Lamb with Ethiopian Collard Greens (bottom).

1 3 5 7 9 10 8 6 4 2

CONTENTS

INTRODUCTION

Entertaining with food and music is integral to African social life, and family, friends and festivity are closely associated in both rural and urban homes. "No advance notice required" is an attitude that prevails, and, in fact, cooking only for the members of your household can get you a bad reputation! So, many hosts and hostesses make it their business to be sure that there are always extra tidbits around for unexpected visitors who might drop in at any time.

Rigid recipes are rare; most African cooks inherit vague techniques by word of mouth and then go on to develop their skills by experimenting with different ingredients and cooking methods. They often create new and interesting combinations by following their instincts rather than written instructions. Cooking in Africa, then, really does come from the heart.

In some African countries, soup is the whole meal, made using meat or fish and dried beans or vegetables and served with a staple food such as *fu fu* (ground rice) or boiled yam. Main courses are dominated by tasty and interesting fish and shellfish, which is found in abundance along the coast or by lakes. There are more than 200 types of fish in Nigeria alone. In some regions, meat and fish are scarce and only eaten on festive occasions, but economic constraints do not prevent Africa's many gourmets from creating very delectable dishes. Meat is usually cooked in spicy sauces, and is frequently flavored with smoked fish or dried prawns.

Throughout Africa, vegetable, bean and lentil dishes are very popular, and meat is often used as one of a number of flavorings, rather than as a main ingredient. For dessert or snacks throughout the day, there is a wonderful array of tropical fruits such as mangoes and papaya, which are a familiar sight.

Eating in Africa is a unique and exciting experience, shaped by local traditions and customs that makes cooking fun and experimental. For above all, cooking the African way is about having a feel for the food.

Opposite: Tropical Fruit Pancakes, and Papaya and Mango with Mango Cream.

Morocco
Sierra Leone
Ghana
Nigeria
Cameroon
Ethiopia
Kenya
Tanzania
Mozambique

INGREDIENTS

There are many ingredients that are used in African cooking that may be unfamiliar. Most, however, can be found in large super-markets, street markets and in African and Asian stores, which often carry a huge variety of fresh fruit and vegetables.

One of the most common flavors to be found is that of the chili, which is often used to add spice to a recipe. The potency of this ingredient varies dramatically, with one of the hottest

Above (clockwise from top left): yams, okra, christophene, sweet potatoes. Above right: mung beans, black-eyed beans, cardamom pods (just showing), egusi, ground egusi.

chilies being the Scotch Bonnet. Even adventurous cooks should accustom themselves slowly to the zingingly hot dishes in which Africans revel! If you do not want fiery food, remove the seeds and core of chilies and add to foods little by little.

Less well-known are the oils, such as palm oil, which is unlike any other oil and should be used sparingly – its distinctive, strong flavor is an acquired taste. Peanut oil is also essential if you want to achieve an authentic African taste, while groundnut paste is used to make sauces or the delicious Groundnut Soup. If the paste is difficult to find, replace it with natural smooth or crunchy peanut butter. Careful experimentation is the key to enjoying these ingredients.

African cooks prepare lots of recipes using vegetables and pulses, and for many people these are the mainstay of their diet.

Yams and sweet potatoes are some of the staple vegetables that make superb dishes. They come in many shapes and sizes and the flesh is either yellow or white. Plantains, members of the banana family, are also essential. All of these are delicious boiled, roasted, baked, mashed or made into chips, and are enjoyed in both sweet and savory dishes.

There are also many other commonly enjoyed vegetables. Christophene is pear-shaped with a cream-colored or green skin. It has a bland flavor, similar to squash. Alternatively, cassava is a tropical vegetable with tuberous roots, brown skin and hard starchy white flesh. Dried and ground, it makes cassava flour and gari, a flour used in various recipes. Egusi, which is also ground and added to many dishes, is made from either melon seed or the seeds of a fruit that is a cross between a gourd and a pumpkin. Eggplant and okra are also popular. Choose small firm okra when you are shopping, and remember to wash and dry them before trimming and cutting, as this will prevent them from becoming too sticky.

Pulses are common in most recipes. Black-eyes peas, for example, originally came fom Africa where they are a staple food. They can be soaked overnight or boiled without soaking, if an extra half hour is added to the cooking time. They are used in all sorts of soups, stews, rice dishes, salads and snacks. Also there are mung beans, sometimes known as green or goden gram which are small, bright green dried beans. Red kidney beans are

Above: A selection of green bananas and plantains.

also common. Care should be taken when preparing these in particular: they can be poisonous when raw and should be soaked for several hours or overnight, and then boiled rapidly for ten to fifteen minutes before simmering until tender, or cooked according to the recipe.

Market stalls are full of luscious fruit – pineapples, coconuts, mangoes and spicy-smelling guavas – and it is not unusual for fruit trees to grow in people's gardens, there just for the picking. Herbs such as cilantro and spices such as allspice add an extra dimension, so that traditional African cuisine makes for an interesting and delicious culinary adventure.

VEGETABLE SOUP WITH COCONUT

The mild, creamy flavor of coconut makes this a vegetable soup for everyone to enjoy all year round. Creamed coconut comes in a block and is usually sold frozen in Asian markets.

INGREDIENTS

6 ounces each, turnip, sweet potato and pumpkin
2 tablespoons butter or margarine
½ red onion, finely chopped
1 teaspoon dried marjoram
½ teaspoon ground ginger
¼ teaspoon ground cinnamon
1 tablespoon chopped scallion
4 cups vegetable stock
2 tablespoons flaked almonds
1 fresh chili, seeded and chopped
1 teaspoon sugar
1 ounce creamed coconut
salt and freshly ground black pepper
chopped cilantro (optional)

SERVES 4

1 Peel the turnip, sweet potato and pumpkin. Chop into medium dice.

2 Melt the butter in a large nonstick saucepan. Add the onion and fry for 4–5 minutes. Add the diced vegetables and fry for 3–4 minutes.

3 Add the marjoram, ginger, cinnamon, scallion, salt and pepper to the pan. Fry over low heat for about 10 minutes, stirring frequently.

4 Add the vegetable stock, flaked almonds, chopped chili and sugar and stir well to mix, then cover and simmer gently for 10–15 minutes, or until all the vegetables are just tender.

5 Grate the creamed coconut into the soup and stir to mix. Sprinkle with chopped cilantro, if desired, then spoon into warmed bowls and serve.

PLANTAIN AND CORN SOUP

P lantains are a very popular ingredient in African cooking, and here they combine with corn to make a hearty soup.

INGREDIENTS
2 tablespoons butter or margarine
1 onion, finely chopped
1 garlic clove, crushed
10 ounces yellow plantains, peeled
and sliced
1 large tomato, peeled and chopped
1 cup corn
1 teaspoon dried tarragon, crushed
3¾ cups vegetable or chicken stock
1 green chili, seeded and chopped
pinch of grated nutmeg
salt and freshly ground black pepper

SERVES 4

1 Melt the butter in a saucepan over medium heat, add the onion and garlic and fry for a few minutes, until the onion is soft.

2 Add the plantain, tomato and corn and cook for 5 minutes.

3 Add the dried tarragon, vegetable or chicken stock, chili and salt and pepper, and simmer for 10 minutes, or until the plantain is tender. Stir in the nutmeg and serve immediately.

GROUNDNUT SOUP

Groundnuts (or peanuts), are very widely used in sauces in African cooking. You'll find groundnut paste in health food stores – it makes a wonderfully rich soup, but you could use peanut butter instead if you prefer. Traditionally the okra are chopped, which gives the soup a slightly "sticky" consistency.

INGREDIENTS
3 tablespoons pure groundnut paste
or peanut butter
6 cups stock
or water
2 tablespoons tomato paste
1 onion, chopped
2 slices fresh ginger
1/4 teaspoon dried thyme
1 bay leaf
salt and cayenne pepper
8 ounces white yam, diced
10 small okra, trimmed (optional)

SERVES 4

1 Place the groundnut paste in a mixing bowl and pour in 1¼ cups of the stock and the tomato paste. Blend together to make a smooth paste.

2 Spoon the nut mixture into a saucepan and add the onion, ginger, thyme, bay leaf, salt, cayenne and the remaining stock.

3 Heat gently until simmering, then cook for 1 hour, stirring occasionally to prevent the nut mixture from sticking.

4 Add the white yam cubes and cook for 10 more minutes. Add the okra, if using, and simmer until the yam and okra are tender. Serve immediately.

LAMB, BEAN AND PUMPKIN SOUP

Black-eyed peas can be bought in health food stores and most supermarkets. Soak them overnight before preparing this tasty soup.

INGREDIENTS

*4 ounces split black-eyed peas,
soaked overnight*

*1¹/₂lb neck of lamb for stew, cut into
medium-size chunks*

*1 teaspoon chopped fresh thyme, or
¹/₂ teaspoon dried*

2 bay leaves

5 cups stock or water

1 onion, sliced

8 ounces pumpkin, diced

2 black cardamom pods

1¹/₂ teaspoons ground turmeric

1 tablespoon chopped cilantro

¹/₂ teaspoon caraway seeds

1 fresh green chili, seeded and chopped

2 green bananas

1 carrot

salt and freshly ground black pepper

SERVES 4

1 Drain the black-eyed peas thoroughly, place them in a saucepan and cover them with fresh cold water.

2 Bring the beans to a boil, boil rapidly for 10 minutes and then reduce the heat and simmer, covered, for 40–50 minutes, until tender, adding more water if necessary. Remove from the heat and set aside to cool.

3 Meanwhile, put the lamb in a large saucepan, add the thyme, bay leaves and stock and bring to a boil. Cover and simmer over medium heat for 1 hour, or until tender.

4 Add the onion, pumpkin, cardamom pods, turmeric, cilantro, caraway, chili and seasoning and stir. Bring back to a simmer and then cook, uncovered, for 15 minutes, until the pumpkin is tender, stirring occasionally.

5 When the peas are cool, spoon them into a blender or food processor with their liquid and blend to a smooth purée.

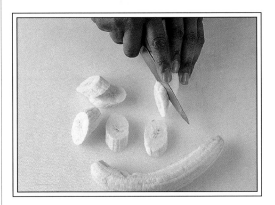

6 Cut the bananas into medium slices and the carrot into thin slices. Stir into the soup with the black-eyed peas and cook for 10–12 minutes, until the vegetables are tender. Adjust the seasoning and serve.

YAM BALLS

Yam balls are a popular snack in many African countries. They are traditionally made quite plain, but can be flavored with chopped vegetables and herbs, as in this recipe, or with cooked meat or fish, or with spices.

INGREDIENTS

1 pound yam, preferably white
2 tablespoons finely chopped onion
3 tablespoons chopped tomatoes
1/2 teaspoon chopped fresh thyme
1 green chili, finely chopped
1 tablespoon finely chopped scallion
1 garlic clove, crushed
1 egg, beaten
oil, for shallow frying
seasoned flour, for dusting
salt and freshly ground black pepper
lettuce, to serve

MAKES ABOUT 24 BALLS

1 Peel the yam, cut it into pieces and boil in salted water for about 30 minutes, or until tender. Drain and mash.

2 Add the onion, tomatoes, thyme, chili, scallion and garlic, then stir in the egg and seasoning and mix well.

3 Using a dessert spoon, scoop the mixture out and mold it into balls. Heat some oil in a frying pan, roll the balls in seasoned flour and then fry for a few minutes, in batches, until golden brown. Drain on paper towels. Serve hot on a bed of lettuce.

COOK'S TIP
If you like, add fresh chopped herbs to the yam mixture; parsley and chives make a good combination. Mix in 2 tablespoons with the egg and seasoning.

TATALE

 verripe plantains are never thrown away, and in Ghana they are often used to make this delicious snack.

INGREDIENTS
2 overripe plantains
2–4 tablespoons self-rising flour
1 small onion, finely chopped
1 egg, beaten
1 teaspoon palm oil (optional)
salt
1 fresh green chili, seeded and chopped
oil, for shallow frying
watercress, to garnish

SERVES 4

1 Peel and mash the plantains. Place them in a bowl and add enough flour to bind, stirring thoroughly.

2 Add the onion, egg, palm oil, if using, salt and chili. Mix well and let stand for 20 minutes.

3 Heat some oil in a frying pan. Spoon in teaspoonfuls of mixture and fry in batches for 3–4 minutes, until golden, turning once. Drain on paper towels. Serve hot or cold, garnished with watercress.

SPICY KEBABS

These spicy kebabs taste wonderful on their own, or you could serve them with a spicy dip.

INGREDIENTS

1 pound ground beef

1 egg

3 garlic cloves, crushed

½ onion, finely chopped

½ teaspoon freshly ground black pepper

1½ teaspoons ground cumin

1½ teaspoons dhania (ground coriander)

1 teaspoon ground ginger

2 teaspoons garam masala

1 tablespoon lemon juice

1–1½ cups fresh white bread crumbs

1 small chili, seeded and chopped

oil, for deep frying

salt and freshly ground black pepper

lettuce leaves, to serve

MAKES 18–20 BALLS

1 Place the ground beef in a large bowl and add the egg, garlic, onion, spices, seasoning, lemon juice, about 1 cup of the bread crumbs and the chili.

2 Using your hands or a wooden spoon, combine the ingredients until the mixture is firm. If it feels sticky, add more of the bread crumbs and mix again until firm.

3 Heat the oil in a large heavy pan or deep-fat fryer. Shape the mixture into balls or fingers and fry, a few at a time, for 5 minutes or until well browned all over.

4 Using a slotted spoon, drain the kebabs and then transfer to a plate lined with paper towels. Cook the remaining kebabs in the same way and then serve them all on a bed of lettuce leaves.

EAST AFRICAN ROAST CHICKEN

A spicy marinade turns a chicken into something very special – serve with rice and a fresh salad for a complete meal.

INGREDIENTS
1 chicken (4–4½ pounds)
2 tablespoons softened butter, plus extra for basting
3 garlic cloves, crushed
1 teaspoon freshly ground black pepper
1 teaspoon ground turmeric
½ teaspoon ground cumin
1 teaspoon dried thyme
1 tablespoon finely chopped cilantro
¼ cup thick coconut milk
¼ cup medium-dry sherry
1 teaspoon tomato paste
salt and cayenne pepper
sprigs of cilantro, to garnish

SERVES 6

1 Remove the giblets from the chicken, if necessary, then rinse out the cavity and pat the skin dry.

2 Put the butter and all the remaining ingredients in a bowl and mix together to form a thick paste.

3 Gently ease the skin of the chicken away from the flesh and rub generously with the herb and butter mixture. Rub more of the mixture over the skin, legs and wings of the chicken and into the neck cavity.

4 Place the chicken in a roasting pan, cover loosely with foil and marinate overnight in the fridge.

5 Preheat the oven to 375°F. Cover the chicken with clean foil and roast for 1 hour, then turn the chicken over and baste with the pan juices. Cover again with foil and cook for 30 minutes.

6 Remove the foil and place the chicken breast-side up. Rub it with extra butter and roast for another 10–15 minutes, until the meat juices run clear and the skin is golden brown. Serve, garnished with plenty of cilantro.

YASSA CHICKEN

S enegalese cooks make wonderful *Yassa*. Instead of frying, they often grill the chicken before adding it to the sauce. For a less tangy flavor, you can add less lemon juice, although it does mellow after cooking.

INGREDIENTS

⅔ cup lemon juice
¼ cup malt vinegar
3 onions, sliced
¼ cup peanut or vegetable oil
2 pounds chicken pieces
2 thyme sprigs
1 green chili, seeded and finely chopped
2 bay leaves
About 2 cups chicken stock

SERVES 4

1 Combine the lemon juice, vinegar, onions and 2 tablespoons of the oil. Place the chicken pieces in a shallow dish and pour the lemon mixture over them. Cover with plastic wrap and let marinate for 3 hours.

2 Heat the remaining oil in a large saucepan and fry the chicken pieces for 4–5 minutes, until browned.

3 Add the marinated onions to the chicken. Fry for 3 minutes, then add the marinade, thyme, chili, bay leaves and half of the stock.

4 Cover the pan and simmer gently over medium heat for about 35 minutes, until the chicken is cooked through, adding more stock as the sauce evaporates. Serve hot.

JOLOFF CHICKEN AND RICE

erve this well-known, colorful West African dish at a dinner party or other special occasion.

INGREDIENTS
1 chicken (2¼ pounds), cut into 4–6
pieces
2 garlic cloves, crushed
1 teaspoon dried thyme
2 tablespoons palm or vegetable oil
1 can (14 ounces) chopped tomatoes
1 tablespoon tomato paste
1 onion, chopped
2 cups chicken stock
or water
2 tablespoons dried shrimp or
crayfish, ground
1 green chili, seeded and finely chopped
1½ cups long-grain
rice, washed
fresh or dried thyme, to garnish

SERVES 4

1 Rub the chicken with the garlic and thyme and set aside.

2 Heat the oil in a saucepan until it begins to smoke and add the tomatoes, tomato paste and onion. Cook over medium-high heat for about 15 minutes, until the tomatoes are reduced, stirring occasionally at first and then more frequently as the tomatoes thicken.

3 Reduce the heat a little, add the chicken pieces and stir well to coat with the sauce. Cook for 10 minutes, stirring, then add the stock, the dried shrimp and the chili. Bring to a boil and simmer for 5 minutes, stirring occasionally.

4 Put the rice in a separate saucepan. Scoop 1¼ cups of the sauce into a measuring cup, add water to make 2 cups and stir into the rice.

5 Cook the rice, covered, until the liquid is absorbed, then place a piece of foil on top of the rice, cover the pan with a lid and cook over low heat for 20 minutes, or until the rice is cooked, adding water if needed.

6 Transfer the chicken pieces to a warmed serving plate. Simmer the sauce until reduced by half. Pour it over the chicken. Serve with the rice, garnished with thyme.

CHICKEN WITH MUNG BEANS

Kuku, this delicious tangy chicken stew, comes from Kenya. The amount of lemon juice can be reduced if you prefer a less sharp sauce.

INGREDIENTS

6 chicken thighs
½ – ⅔ teaspoon ground ginger
2 ounces mung beans
¼ cup corn oil
2 onions, finely chopped
2 garlic cloves, crushed
5 tomatoes, peeled and chopped
1 green chili, seeded and finely chopped
2 tablespoons lemon juice
1 cup coconut milk
1 cup water
1 tablespoon chopped cilantro
salt and freshly ground black pepper
green vegetables, cooked rice and
chapatis, to serve

SERVES 4–6

1 Season the chicken pieces with the ground ginger and a little salt and pepper, then set aside in a cool place to marinate. Meanwhile, boil the mung beans in plenty of water for 35 minutes or until soft, then mash well.

2 Heat the oil in a large saucepan over medium heat and fry the chicken pieces, in batches if necessary, until they are evenly browned. Transfer them to a plate and set aside, reserving the oil and chicken juices in the pan.

3 In the same pan, fry the onions and garlic for 5 minutes, then add the tomatoes and chili and cook for 1–2 minutes longer, stirring well.

4 Add the mashed mung beans, lemon juice and coconut ___ __ e pan. Simmer for 5 minutes, then a__ __ chicken pieces and a little water if the sauce is too thick. Stir in the cilantro and simmer for about 35 minutes, or until the chicken is cooked through. Serve with green vegetables, rice and chapatis.

KOFTA CURRY

lthough fussy, koftas are worth making. You can prepare them in advance and chill until needed.

INGREDIENTS
1 pound ground beef or lamb
3 tablespoons finely chopped onion
1 tablespoon chopped cilantro
1 tablespoon plain yogurt
¼ cup all-purpose flour
2 teaspoons ground cumin
1 teaspoon garam masala
1 teaspoon ground turmeric
1 teaspoon dhania (ground coriander)
1 green chili, seeded and finely chopped
2 garlic cloves, crushed
¼ teaspoon black mustard seeds
1 egg (optional)
salt and freshly ground black pepper

FOR THE CURRY SAUCE
2 tablespoons ghee or butter
1 onion, finely chopped
2 garlic cloves, crushed
3 tablespoons curry powder
4 green cardamom pods
2½ ....en stock
... ...spoon tomato paste
2 tablespoons plain yogurt
1 tablespoon chopped cilantro
cooked rice and cilantro, to serve

SERVES 4

1 Put the ground meat into a large bowl, add all the remaining meatball ingredients and mix well with your hands. Roll the mixture into small balls and set aside on a floured plate until required.

2 To make the curry sauce, heat the ghee in a saucepan over medium heat and fry the chopped onion and garlic for about 10 minutes, or until the onion is soft and buttery.

3 Reduce the heat, then add the curry powder and cardamom pods and cook for a few minutes, stirring well.

4 Slowly stir in the stock, then add the tomato paste, yogurt and cilantro and stir well. Simmer for 10 minutes.

5 Add the koftas a few at a time, cook briefly and then add a few more, until they are all in the pan. Simmer, uncovered, for about 20 minutes, or until the koftas are cooked. Avoid stirring, but gently shake the pan occasionally to move the koftas around.

6 The curry should thicken slightly, but if it is too dry add more stock or water. Serve hot over rice, garnished with cilantro.

LAMB TAGINE WITH CILANTRO AND SPICES

Here is a Moroccan-style tagine. It can be made with chops or cutlets, and either marinated or cooked immediately after seasoning.

INGREDIENTS

4 lamb chops or cutlets
2 garlic cloves, crushed
pinch of saffron strands
½ teaspoon ground cinnamon, plus extra to garnish
½ teaspoon ground ginger
1 tablespoon chopped cilantro
1 tablespoon chopped fresh parsley
1 onion, finely chopped
3 tablespoons olive oil
1 cup lamb stock
½ cup blanched almonds
1 teaspoon sugar
salt and freshly ground black pepper
cooked rice and bread, to serve

SERVES 4

1 Season the lamb with the garlic, saffron, cinnamon, ginger and a little salt and black pepper. Place on a large plate and sprinkle with the cilantro, parsley and onion. Cover loosely and set aside in the fridge for a few hours to marinate.

2 Heat the oil in a large frying pan over medium heat. Add the marinated lamb and all the herbs and onion from the dish.

3 Fry for 1–2 minutes, turning once, then add the stock, bring to a boil and simmer gently for 30 minutes, turning the chops once.

4 Meanwhile, heat a small frying pan over medium heat, add the almonds and dry fry until golden, shaking the pan occasionally to make sure they color evenly. Transfer to a bowl and set aside.

5 Transfer the chops to a serving plate and keep warm. Increase the heat under the pan and boil the sauce until reduced by about half. Stir in the sugar. Pour the sauce over the chops, arrange on a bed of rice and sprinkle with the fried almonds and a little extra ground cinnamon. Serve immediately, with fresh bread to mop up the juices.

COOK'S TIP
Lamb Tagine is a fragrant dish that originated in North Africa. It is traditionally made in a cooking dish known as a tagine, from which it takes its name. This dish consists of a plate with a tall lid with sloping sides. It has a narrow opening to let steam escape, while retaining the flavor.

NIGERIAN MEAT STEW

This recipe was adapted from a Nigerian stew. It is made with meats of different flavors, such as beef, innards and lamb, along with dried fish or snails, and served with yams or rice.

INGREDIENTS

1½ pounds oxtail, chopped

1 pound stewing beef, cubed

1 pound skinless, boneless chicken breasts, chopped

2 garlic cloves, crushed

2 small onions

2 tablespoons palm or vegetable oil

2 tablespoons tomato paste

1 can (14 ounces) plum tomatoes

2 bay leaves

1 teaspoon dried thyme

1 teaspoon pumpkin pie spice

salt and freshly ground black pepper

SERVES 4–6

1 Place the oxtail in a large saucepan, cover with water and bring to a boil. Skim the surface of any froth, then cover and cook for 1½ hours, adding more water as necessary.

2 Add the beef and continue to cook for another hour, until tender.

3 Meanwhile, season the chicken breasts with the crushed garlic and coarsely chop one onion.

4 Heat the oil in a large saucepan over medium heat and fry the chopped onion for about 5 minutes, until soft. Stir in the tomato paste, cook briskly for a few minutes, then add the chicken. Stir well and cook gently for 5 minutes.

5 Meanwhile, place the plum tomatoes and the remaining half onion in a food processor or blender and blend to a paste. Stir into the chicken mixture with the bay leaves, thyme, mixed spice and seasoning.

6 Add about 2½ cups of stock from the cooked oxtail and beef and simmer for 35 minutes.

7 Add the oxtail and beef to the chicken. Heat gently, adjust the seasoning and serve hot.

SPICED FRIED LAMB

An Ethiopian dish, *Awaze Tibs*, is flavored with a red pepper spice mixture called berbiri, which is traditionally made from a variety of East African herbs and spices.

INGREDIENTS
1 pound lamb loin
3 tablespoons olive oil
1 red onion, sliced
½ teaspoon grated fresh ginger
2 garlic cloves, crushed
½ green chili, seeded and finely chopped (optional)
1 tablespoon clarified butter or ghee
salt and freshly ground black pepper
cabbage and red bell pepper strips, to serve

FOR THE BERBIRI
½ teaspoon each chili powder, paprika, ground ginger, ground cinnamon, ground cardamom seeds and dried basil
1 teaspoon garlic powder

SERVES 4

1 To make the berbiri, combine all the ingredients in a small bowl and put into an airtight container. Berbiri will keep for several months if stored in a cool dry place.

2 Trim the meat of any fat and cut into 3/4-inch cubes.

3 Heat the oil in a large frying pan and fry the meat and onion for 5–6 minutes, until the meat is browned on all sides.

4 Add the ginger, garlic and 2 teaspoons of the berbiri to the pan, then stir-fry over high heat for 5–10 minutes more.

5 Add the chili, if using, and season well. Stir in the butter or ghee just before serving with cabbage and red peppers.

MUTTON WITH BLACK-EYED PEAS AND PUMPKIN

Cooking meat together with vegetables, especially beans, is very common in African cooking. The pumpkin brings a lovely sweetness to this dish. Serve it with boiled yams, plantains or sweet potatoes.

INGREDIENTS

*1 pound boneless lean mutton or
lamb, cubed*
4 cups chicken or lamb stock or water
*½ cup black-eyed peas,
soaked overnight*
1 onion, chopped
2 garlic cloves, crushed
2½ tablespoons tomato paste
1½ teaspoons dried thyme
1½ teaspoons palm or vegetable oil
1 teaspoon pumpkin pie spice
½ teaspoon freshly ground black pepper
4 ounces pumpkin, chopped
salt and a little hot pepper sauce

SERVES 4

1 Put the meat in a large pan with the stock and bring to a boil. Skim off any foam, then reduce the heat, cover and simmer for 1 hour.

2 Stir in the drained black-eyed peas and continue cooking for about 35 minutes.

3 Add the onion, garlic, tomato paste, dried thyme, oil, mixed spice, ground black pepper, salt and hot pepper sauce, and cook for another 15 minutes, or until the beans are tender.

4 Add the pumpkin and simmer gently for 10 minutes, until the pumpkin is very soft or almost mushy.

COOK'S TIP

Mutton is a mature meat with a very good flavor and texture, ideal for stews and casseroles. If mutton is not available, lamb makes a good substitute. Any dried white beans can be used instead of black-eyed peas. If a firmer texture is preferred, cook the pumpkin for about 5 minutes, until just tender.

FISH AND SHRIMP WITH SPINACH AND COCONUT

Fresh fish is combined with an unusual shrimp sauce to make a truly superb African dish.

INGREDIENTS
1 pound white fish fillets (cod or haddock)
1 tablespoon lemon or lime juice
1/2 teaspoon garlic powder
1 teaspoon ground cinnamon
1/2 teaspoon dried thyme
1/2 teaspoon paprika
1/2 teaspoon freshly ground black pepper
salt
seasoned flour, for dusting
vegetable oil, for shallow frying

FOR THE SAUCE
2 tablespoons butter or margarine
1 onion, finely chopped
1 garlic clove, crushed
1 cup coconut milk
4 ounces fresh spinach, finely sliced
8–10 ounces cooked, peeled shrimp
1 red chili, seeded and finely chopped

SERVES 4

1 Place the fish in a shallow bowl and sprinkle with the lemon juice.

2 Stir together the garlic powder, ground cinnamon, dried thyme, paprika, pepper and salt, and sprinkle it over the fish. Cover loosely with plastic wrap and allow to marinate in a cool place or put in the fridge for a few hours.

3 Meanwhile, make the sauce. Melt the butter in a large saucepan and fry the onion and garlic for 5–6 minutes, until the onion is soft, stirring frequently.

4 Place the coconut milk and spinach in a separate saucepan and bring to a boil. Cook gently for a few minutes, until the spinach has wilted and the coconut milk has reduced a little, then set the mixture aside to cool slightly.

5 Blend the spinach mixture in a blender or food processor for 30 seconds and add to the onion with the shrimp and chopped red chili. Stir well and simmer gently for a few minutes, then set aside while cooking the fish fillets.

6 Using a sharp knife, cut the marinated fish into 2-inch pieces and dip in the seasoned flour. Heat a little oil in a large frying pan and fry the fish pieces, in batches if necessary, for 2–3 minutes on each side, until golden brown. Drain on paper towels.

7 Arrange the fish on a warmed serving plate. Gently reheat the sauce and serve separately in a sauceboat or pour it over the fish fillets.

TILAPIA IN TURMERIC, MANGO AND TOMATO SAUCE

T ilapia can be found in most fish markets. Serve this dish with yams or boiled yellow plantains.

INGREDIENTS

4 tilapia

1/2 lemon

2 garlic cloves, crushed

1/2 teaspoon dried thyme

2 tablespoons chopped scallions

vegetable oil, for shallow frying

flour, for dusting

2 tablespoons peanut oil

1 tablespoon butter or margarine

1 onion, finely chopped

3 tomatoes, peeled and finely chopped

1 teaspoon ground turmeric

1/2 cup white wine

1 green chili, seeded and finely chopped

2 cups fish stock

1 teaspoon sugar

1 underripe mango, peeled and diced

salt and freshly ground black pepper

1 tablespoon chopped fresh parsley,
to garnish

SERVES 4

1 Place the fish in a shallow bowl, squeeze the lemon juice over it and gently rub in the garlic, thyme and some salt and pepper.

2 Place some of the scallion in the cavity of each fish, cover with plastic wrap and let marinate for a few hours.

3 Heat some oil in a frying pan, coat the fish with flour, then fry on both sides for a few minutes, until golden brown. Remove with a slotted spoon and set aside.

4 Heat the peanut oil and butter in a saucepan and fry the onion for 4–5 minutes, until soft. Stir in the tomatoes and cook briskly for a few minutes.

5 Add the turmeric, wine, chili, fish stock and sugar, stir well and bring to a boil, then simmer gently, covered, for 10 minutes.

6 Add the fish and cook over low heat for 15–20 minutes, until the fish is cooked. Arrange the mango around the fish and cook for 1–2 minutes to heat through.

7 Arrange the fish on a warmed serving plate with the mango and tomato sauce poured over it. Garnish with chopped parsley and serve immediately.

TANZANIAN FISH CURRY

This delicious fish curry from Tanzania in East Africa is a national favorite, and the abundance of fish available means that it is often on the menu.

INGREDIENTS
1 large red snapper
1 lemon
3 tablespoons vegetable oil
1 onion, finely chopped
2 garlic cloves, crushed
3 tablespoons curry powder
1 can (14 ounces) chopped tomatoes
1 heaped tablespoon smooth peanut butter,
preferably unsalted
1/2 green bell pepper, chopped
2 slices fresh ginger
1 green chili, seeded and finely chopped
about 2 cups fish stock
1 tablespoon finely chopped
cilantro
salt and freshly ground black pepper

SERVES 2–3

1 Season the fish, inside and out, with salt and pepper and place in a shallow bowl. Halve the lemon and squeeze the juice all over the fish. Cover loosely with plastic wrap and let marinate for at least 2 hours.

2 Heat the oil in a large nonstick saucepan and fry the onion and garlic for 5–6 minutes, until soft. Reduce the heat, add the curry powder and cook, stirring, for 5 minutes longer.

3 Stir in the tomatoes and the peanut butter, mixing well, then add the green pepper, ginger, chili and stock. Stir well and simmer gently for 10 minutes.

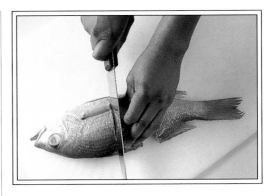

4 Cut the fish into pieces and gently lower into the sauce. Simmer for 20 minutes, or until the fish is cooked through, then, using a slotted spoon, transfer the fish pieces to a plate.

5 Stir the cilantro into the sauce and adjust the seasoning. If the sauce is very thick, add a little extra stock or water. Return the fish to the sauce, cook gently to heat through and serve immediately.

COOK'S TIP
The fish can be fried before adding to the sauce, if preferred. Dip in seasoned flour and fry in oil in a pan or a wok for a few minutes before adding to the sauce.

BAKED RED SNAPPER

You can vary the amount of sauce to serve with this dish each time you make it – for less sauce, just remove the foil after cooking for 20 minutes and continue baking, uncovered.

INGREDIENTS
1 large red snapper, cleaned
juice of 1 lemon
1/2 teaspoon paprika
1/2 teaspoon garlic powder
1/2 teaspoon dried thyme
1/2 teaspoon freshly ground black pepper
cooked rice and lemon wedges, to serve

FOR THE SAUCE
2 tablespoons palm or vegetable oil
1 onion
1 can (14 ounces) chopped tomatoes
2 garlic cloves
1 thyme sprig or 1/2 teaspoon dried thyme
1 green chili, seeded and finely chopped
1/2 green bell pepper, seeded and chopped
1 cup fish stock, bottled clam juice or water

SERVES 3–4

1 Preheat the oven to 400°F. For the sauce, heat the oil in a saucepan, fry the onion for 5 minutes, then add the tomatoes, garlic, thyme and chili.

2 Add the green pepper and fish stock. Bring to a boil, stirring, then reduce the heat and simmer, covered, for about 10 minutes, or until the vegetables are soft. Allow to cool a little and then transfer to a blender or food processor and blend to a smooth paste.

3 Wash the fish well and score the skin with a sharp knife in a criss-cross pattern. Combine the lemon juice, paprika, garlic, thyme and black pepper, spoon over the fish and rub in well.

4 Place the fish in a greased baking dish and pour the sauce over the top. Cover with foil and bake for 30–40 minutes, or until the fish is cooked and flakes easily when tested with a knife. Serve with boiled rice and lemon wedges.

FRIED POMFRET IN COCONUT SAUCE

 Once again, the distinctive flavor of coconut is used to make this an African dish to remember.

INGREDIENTS
4 pomfret or porgy
1 lemon
1 teaspoon garlic powder
vegetable oil, for shallow frying
salt and freshly ground black pepper

FOR THE COCONUT SAUCE
2 cups water
2 thin slices fresh ginger
1–1½ ounces creamed coconut
2 tablespoons vegetable oil
1 red onion, sliced
2 garlic cloves, crushed
1 green chili, seeded and thinly sliced
1 tablespoon chopped cilantro

SERVES 4

1 Cut the fish in half and sprinkle inside and out with the juice from the lemon. Season with the garlic powder and salt and pepper. Allow to marinate for a few hours.

2 Heat a little oil in a large frying pan. Pat away the excess lemon juice from the fish, then fry in the oil for 10 minutes, turning once. Set aside.

3 To make the sauce, place the water in a saucepan with the slices of ginger, bring to a boil and simmer until the liquid is reduced to just over 1 cup. Take out the ginger and reserve, then add the creamed coconut to the pan and stir until the coconut has melted.

4 Heat the oil in a wok or large pan and fry the onion and garlic for 2–3 minutes. Add the reserved ginger and coconut stock, the chili and cilantro, stir well and then gently add the fish. Simmer for 10 minutes, until the fish is cooked through.

5 Transfer the fish to a warmed serving plate, adjust the seasoning for the sauce and pour it over the fish. Serve immediately.

DONU'S LOBSTER PIRI PIRI

obster in its shell, in true Nigerian style, flavored with a dried shrimp piri piri sauce.

INGREDIENTS
1/4 cup vegetable oil
2 onions, chopped
1 teaspoon chopped fresh ginger
1 pound fresh or canned
tomatoes, chopped
1 tablespoon tomato paste
8 ounces cooked, peeled shrimp
2 teaspoons ground coriander
1 green chili, seeded and chopped
1 tablespoon ground dried shrimp
or crayfish
2 cups water
1 green bell pepper, seeded and sliced
2 cooked lobsters, halved
salt and freshly ground black pepper
cilantro sprigs, to garnish
cooked rice, to serve

SERVES 2–4

1 Heat the oil in a large nonstick saucepan and fry the onions, ginger, tomatoes and tomato paste for 5 minutes, or until the onions are soft.

2 Add the shrimp, ground coriander, chili and ground shrimp and stir well to combine.

3 Stir in the water, green pepper and salt and pepper, bring to a boil and simmer, uncovered, over medium heat for about 20–30 minutes, until the sauce is reduced.

4 Add the lobsters to the sauce and cook for a few minutes to heat through. Arrange each lobster half on a bed of fluffy white rice and top with the sauce. Garnish with cilantro and serve immediately.

EGUSI SPINACH AND EGG

This is a superbly balanced dish for vegetarians. Egusi, or ground melon seed, is widely used in West African cooking. It adds a creamy texture and a nutty flavor to many recipes and is especially good with fresh spinach.

INGREDIENTS

2 pounds fresh spinach
¼ cup egusi
6 tablespoons peanut or vegetable oil
4 tomatoes, peeled and chopped
1 onion, chopped
2 garlic cloves, crushed
1 slice fresh ginger, finely chopped
⅔ cup vegetable stock
1 red chili, seeded and finely chopped
6 eggs
salt

SERVES 4

COOK'S TIP
Instead of using hard-cooked eggs, you could make an omelet flavored with herbs and garlic. Serve it either whole, or sliced, with the egusi sauce. If you can't find egusi, use ground almonds as a substitute.

1 Roll the spinach into bundles and cut into strips. Place in a bowl.

2 Cover the spinach with boiling water, then drain through a strainer. Press with your fingers to remove excess water.

3 Place the *egusi* in a bowl and gradually add enough water to form a paste, stirring constantly.

4 Heat the oil in a saucepan, add the tomatoes, onion, garlic and ginger and fry over medium heat for 10 minutes, stirring frequently.

5 Add the *egusi* paste, stock, chili and salt, cook for 10 minutes, then add the spinach and stir into the sauce. Cook for 15 minutes, uncovered, stirring frequently.

6 Meanwhile, hard-cook the eggs, stand in cold water for a few minutes to cool, then shell and cut in half. Arrange in a shallow serving dish and pour the *egusi* spinach over the top. Serve hot.

MAKANDE

 A traditional dish from Uparie-Tanzania that can be served with meat, fish or simply a salad.

INGREDIENTS

1 cup red kidney beans,
soaked overnight
1 onion, chopped
2 garlic cloves, crushed
3 ounces creamed coconut
1 cup frozen corn
1 cup vegetable stock
or water
salt and freshly ground black pepper

SERVES 3–4

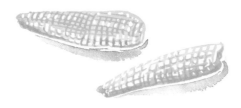

1 Drain the kidney beans and place in a pan. Cover the beans with water and boil rapidly for 15 minutes. Reduce the heat and continue boiling for about 1 hour, until the beans are tender, adding more water if necessary. Drain and discard the cooking liquid.

2 Place the beans in a clean pan with the onion, garlic, coconut, corn and salt and pepper.

3 Add the stock, bring to a boil and simmer for 20 minutes, stirring occasionally to dissolve the coconut.

4 Adjust the seasoning and spoon into a warmed serving dish.

VEGETABLES IN PEANUT SAUCE

Palm oil, a much-used African ingredient, gives this dish a distinctive flavor; if you prefer, however, you can use a milder oil.

INGREDIENTS

1 tablespoon palm or vegetable oil
1 onion, chopped
2 garlic cloves, crushed
1 can (14 ounces) tomatoes, puréed
3 tablespoons smooth peanut butter, preferably unsalted
2½ cups water
1 teaspoon dried thyme
1 green chili, seeded and chopped
1 vegetable stock cube
½ teaspoon ground allspice
salt
2 carrots
4 ounces white cabbage
6 ounces okra
½ red bell pepper
⅔ cup vegetable stock

SERVES 4

1 Heat the oil in a large nonstick saucepan and fry the onion and garlic over medium heat for 5 minutes, stirring frequently. Add the tomatoes and peanut butter and stir well.

2 Stir in the water, thyme, chili, stock cube, allspice and a little salt. Bring to a boil, then simmer gently, uncovered, for about 35 minutes.

3 Meanwhile, cut the carrots into sticks, slice the cabbage, remove the ends from the okra and seed and slice the red pepper.

4 Place the vegetables in a saucepan with the stock, bring to a boil and cook until tender but still with a little bite.

5 Drain the vegetables and place them in a warmed serving dish. Pour the peanut sauce over the top and serve.

CHICK-PEAS, SWEET POTATO AND GARDEN EGG

G arden egg is a small variety of eggplant used widely in West Africa. It is round and white, which may explain its other name – eggplant.

INGREDIENTS
3 tablespoons olive oil
1 red onion, chopped
3 garlic cloves, crushed
1 small sweet potato, peeled and diced
3 garden eggs or 1 large eggplant, diced
1 can (15 ounces) chick-peas, drained
1 teaspoon dried tarragon
1/2 teaspoon dried thyme
1 teaspoon ground cumin
1 teaspoon ground turmeric
1/2 teaspoon ground allspice
5 canned plum tomatoes, chopped with
1/4 cup reserved juice
6 dried apricots
2 1/2 cups vegetable stock
1 green chili, seeded and finely chopped
2 tablespoons chopped cilantro
salt and freshly ground black pepper

SERVES 3–4

1 Heat the olive oil in a large pan over medium heat. Add the onion, garlic and sweet potatoes and cook for about 5 minutes, until the onion is slightly softened.

2 Stir in the garden eggs then add the chick-peas and the herbs and spices. Stir well to mix and cook over a gentle heat for few minutes.

3 Add the tomatoes and their juice, the apricots, stock, chili and seasoning. Stir well, bring slowly to a boil and cook for about 15 minutes.

4 When the sweet potatoes are tender, add the cilantro, stir and adjust the seasoning, if necessary, and serve.

BEAN AND GARI LOAF

 T his recipe is a newly created vegetarian dish using typical Ghanaian flavors and ingredients.

INGREDIENTS
*1 cup red kidney beans,
soaked overnight
1 tablespoon butter or margarine
1 onion, finely chopped
2 garlic cloves, crushed
¹/₂ red bell pepper, seeded and chopped
¹/₂ green bell pepper, seeded and chopped
1 green chili, seeded and finely chopped
1 teaspoon mixed chopped herbs
2 eggs
1 tablespoon lemon juice
5 tablespoons gari
salt and freshly ground black pepper*

SERVES 4

COOK'S TIP
Gari is a coarse-grained flour used as a staple food, in a similar way to ground rice. It is made from a starchy root vegetable, cassava, which is first dried, then ground.

---

1 Drain the beans, place in a pan, cover with water and boil for 15 minutes. Reduce the heat and boil for 1 hour, or until the beans are tender. Drain, reserving the cooking liquid. Grease a 2-pound loaf pan and preheat the oven to 375°F.

2 Melt the butter and fry the onion, garlic and peppers for 5 minutes. Add the chili, herbs and seasoning.

3 Place the cooked kidney beans in a bowl and mash to a pulp. Add the onion and pepper mixture and stir well. Cool slightly, then stir in the eggs and lemon juice.

4 Place the gari in a separate bowl and sprinkle generously with warm water. The gari should become soft and fluffy after about 5 minutes.

5 Pour the gari into the bean and onion mixture and stir together thoroughly. If the consistency is too stiff, add a little of the bean liquid. Spoon the mixture into the prepared loaf pan and bake for 35–45 minutes, until firm to the touch. ✦

6 Cool the loaf in the pan before turning it out onto a plate. Cut into thick slices and serve.

BLACK-EYED PEA STEW WITH SPICY PUMPKIN

This colorful African stew has a wonderfully spicy flavor that cheers up a cold winter's day.

INGREDIENTS

1 cup black-eyed peas, soaked overnight and drained

1 onion, chopped

1 pepper, seeded and chopped

2 garlic cloves, crushed

1 vegetable stock cube

1 fresh thyme sprig

1 teaspoon paprika

¹/₂ teaspoon pumpkin pie spice

2 carrots, sliced

1–2 tablespoons palm oil

1¹/₂ pounds pumpkin

1 onion

2 tablespoons butter or margarine

2 garlic cloves, crushed

3 tomatoes, peeled and chopped

¹/₂ teaspoon ground cinnamon

2 teaspoons curry powder

pinch of grated nutmeg

²/₃ cup water

salt, hot pepper sauce and freshly ground black pepper

SERVES 3–4

1 Bring the beans to a boil, then add the onion, pepper, garlic, stock cube, thyme, paprika and mixed spice. Simmer for 45 minutes, or until the beans are tender. Season with salt and a little hot pepper

2 Add the carrots and palm oil and continue cooking for 10–12 minutes or until the carrots are cooked, adding a little more water if necessary. Remove from the heat and set aside.

3 To make the spicy pumpkin, cut the pumpkin into cubes and finely chop the onion.

4 Melt the butter in a frying pan or saucepan, then add the pumpkin, onion, garlic, tomatoes, spices and water. Stir well to combine and simmer until the pumpkin is soft. Season with salt, hot pepper sauce and black pepper, to taste. Serve with the cooked black-eyed peas.

BULGUR AND PINE NUT PILAF

P ilaf is a popular staple in the Middle East, and this is a North African version. Serve it with a vegetable or meat stew to make a truly satisfying meal.

INGREDIENTS

2 tablespoons olive oil

1 onion, chopped

1 garlic clove, crushed

1 teaspoon ground saffron or turmeric

1/2 teaspoon ground cinnamon

1 green chili, seeded and chopped

2 cups vegetable stock

2/3 cup white wine

1 1/3 cups bulgur

1 tablespoon butter or margarine

2–3 tablespoons pine nuts

2 tablespoons chopped fresh parsley

SERVES 4

1 Heat the olive oil in a large saucepan and fry the onion until soft. Add the garlic, ground saffron or turmeric, cinnamon and chili and fry for a few more seconds.

2 Add the stock and wine, bring to a boil, then simmer for 8 minutes.

3 Rinse the bulgur under cold water, drain and add to the stock. Cover and simmer gently for about 15 minutes, until the stock is absorbed.

4 Melt the butter or margarine in a small pan, add the pine nuts and fry for a few minutes, until golden. Add to the bulgur with the chopped parsley and stir with a fork to mix.

5 Spoon into a warmed serving dish and serve hot.

COOK'S TIP
You can leave out the wine, if you prefer, and replace it with water or stock. It's not essential, but it adds extra flavor.

CAMEROON COCONUT RICE

T his version of a favorite African dish, Coconut Joloff, can be left moist, like a risotto, or cooked longer for drier results.

INGREDIENTS
2 tablespoons vegetable oil
1 onion, chopped
2 tablespoons tomato paste
2¹/₂ cups coconut milk
2 carrots
1 yellow bell pepper
1 teaspoon dried thyme
¹/₂ teaspoon pumkin pie spice
1 fresh green chili, seeded and chopped
1¹/₂ cups long-grain rice
salt
shredded coconut, to garnish

SERVES 4

1 Heat the oil in a large saucepan and fry the onion for 2 minutes. Add the tomato purée and cook over medium heat for 5–6 minutes, stirring constantly. Add the coconut milk, stir well and bring to a boil.

2 Coarsely chop the carrots and chop the pepper, discarding the seeds.

3 Stir the carrots, pepper, thyme, pumpkin pie spice, chili and rice into the onion mixture, season with salt and bring to a boil. Cover and cook over low heat until the rice has absorbed most of the liquid. Cover the rice with foil, secure with the lid and steam very gently until the rice is done. Serve hot, garnished with coconut shreds.

KENYAN MUNG BEAN STEW

The Kenyan name for this simple and tasty stew made from dried mung beans is *Dengu*.

INGREDIENTS
1 cup mung beans,
soaked overnight
2 tablespoons ghee or butter
2 garlic cloves, crushed
1 red onion, chopped
2 tablespoons tomato paste
½ green bell pepper, seeded and cut into
small cubes
½ red bell pepper, seeded and cut into
small cubes
1 green chili, seeded and finely chopped
1¼ cups water

SERVES 4

COOK'S TIP
If you prefer a more traditional, smoother texture, cook the mung beans until very soft, then mash them thoroughly until smooth.

1 Put the mung beans in a large saucepan, cover with water and boil until the beans are soft and the water has evaporated. Remove from the heat and mash coarsely with a fork or potato masher.

2 Heat the ghee or butter in a separate saucepan, add the garlic and onion and fry for 4–5 minutes until golden brown, then add the tomato paste and cook for 2–3 more minutes, stirring constantly.

3 Stir in the mashed beans, then the green and red peppers and chili.

4 Add the water, stirring well to combine the ingredients.

5 Transfer to a clean saucepan and simmer for about 10 minutes, then spoon into a serving dish and serve immediately.

GROUND RICE

 round rice is a staple dish in West Africa, where it is often served with soups and stews.

INGREDIENTS
1¼ cups water
2 tablespoons butter or margarine
1¼ cups milk
½ teaspoon salt
1 tablespoon chopped fresh parsley
1½ cups ground rice

SERVES 4

1 Place the water, butter and milk in a saucepan, bring to a boil and add the salt and parsley.

2 Add the ground rice, stirring vigorously with a wooden spoon to prevent the rice from becoming lumpy.

3 Cover the pan and cook over low heat for about 15 minutes, beating the mixture regularly every two minutes to prevent lumps from forming.

4 To test if the rice is cooked, rub a pinch of the mixture between your fingers; if it feels smooth and fairly dry, it is ready. Serve the rice dish hot.

COOK'S TIP
Ground rice is creamy white and when cooked has a slightly grainy texture. Although often used here in sweet dishes, it is a tasty grain to serve with savory dishes too. The addition of milk makes it creamier.

MANDAZI

S erve this East African bread either as a snack or as an accompaniment to a meal.

INGREDIENTS

4 or 5 cardamom pods
4 cups self-rising flour
3 tablespoons sugar
1 teaspoon baking powder
1 egg, beaten
2 tablespoons vegetable oil, plus extra for deep frying
1 cup milk or water

MAKES ABOUT 15

2 Put the egg and oil in a small bowl and beat together, then add to the flour mixture. Mix with your fingers, gradually adding the milk or water to make a dough.

3 Lightly knead the dough until smooth and not sticky when a finger is pushed into it, adding more flour if necessary. Put in a warm place for 15 minutes.

4 Roll out the dough to about a ½ inch thickness and cut into 2½-inch rounds. Heat the oil and deep fry the mandazis for 4–5 minutes, until golden brown, turning frequently in the oil.

1 Crush each cardamom pod, shake out the seeds and grind them in a small mortar and pestle. Place in a large bowl with the flour, sugar and baking powder. Stir well.

PLANTAIN AND GREEN BANANA SALAD

The plantains and bananas may be cooked in their skins to retain their soft texture. They will then absorb all the flavor of the dressing.

INGREDIENTS

2 firm yellow plantains
3 green bananas
1 garlic clove, crushed
1 red onion
1–2 tablespoons
chopped cilantro
3 tablespoons sunflower oil
1½ tablespoons malt vinegar
salt and freshly ground black pepper

SERVES 4

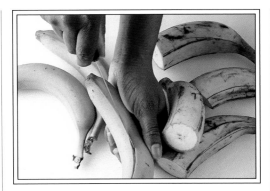

1 Slit the plantains and bananas lengthwise along their natural ridges, then cut in half and place in a large saucepan.

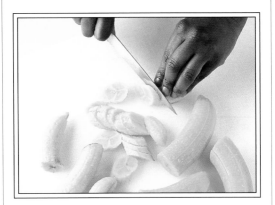

2 Cover the plantains and bananas with water, add a little salt and bring to a boil. Boil gently for 20 minutes, until tender, then remove from the water. When they are cool enough to handle, peel and cut into medium-size slices.

3 Put the plantain and banana slices into a bowl and add the garlic, turning to mix.

4 Halve the onion and slice thinly. Add to the bowl with the cilantro, oil, vinegar and seasoning. Toss together to mix, and then serve.

ETHIOPIAN COLLARD GREENS

Also known as *Abesha Gomen*, this dish is simple and delicious. Use chard or other spring greens in place of the collard greens if you are unable to get the real thing.

INGREDIENTS
1 pound collard greens
4 tablespoons olive oil
2 small red onions, finely chopped
1 garlic clove, crushed
½ teaspoon grated fresh ginger
2 green chilies, seeded and sliced
⅔ cup vegetable stock
or water
1 red bell pepper, seeded and sliced
salt and freshly ground black pepper

SERVES 4

COOK'S TIP
Traditionally, this dish is cooked with more liquid and for longer. Here, the cooking time has been reduced from 45 to 15 minutes. However, if you prefer a more authentic taste, cook for longer and increase the amount of liquid. Green cabbage is a good substitute for collard greens.

1 Wash the collard greens, then strip the leaves from the stalks and steam the leaves over a pan of boiling water for about 5 minutes, until slightly wilted. Set aside on a plate to cool, then place in a strainer or colander and press out the excess water.

2 Using a large, sharp knife, slice the collard greens very thinly.

3 Heat the oil in a saucepan and fry the onions until browned. Add the garlic and ginger and stir-fry with the onions for a few minutes, then add the chilies and a little of the stock and cook for 2 minutes.

4 Add the greens, red pepper and the remaining stock. Season with salt and pepper, mix well, then cover and cook over low heat for about 15 minutes.

GREEN LENTIL
SALAD

A *zifa* is the African name for this piquant, colorful salad. It is best served as an accompaniment to a meat or fish dish.

INGREDIENTS
1 cup green lentils,
soaked overnight
2 tomatoes, peeled and chopped
1 red onion, finely chopped
1 green chili, seeded and chopped
4 tablespoons lemon juice
5 tablespoons olive oil
1/2 teaspoon mustard
salt and freshly ground black pepper
lettuce leaves, to garnish

SERVES 4

1 Drain the lentils and place them in a saucepan, cover with water and bring to a boil. Simmer for 45 minutes or until soft, drain, then tip into a bowl and mash lightly with a potato masher.

2 Add the chopped tomatoes, onion, chili, lemon juice, olive oil, mustard and seasoning. Mix well, adjust the seasoning if necessary, then chill before serving the salad garnished with lettuce leaves.

PAPAYA AND MANGO WITH MANGO CREAM

Mangoes vary tremendously in size. If you can only find small ones, buy three instead of two for this refreshing dessert.

INGREDIENTS

2 large ripe mangoes
1½ cups heavy cream
8 dried apricots, halved
⅔ cup orange juice
or water
1 ripe papaya

SERVES 4

2 Turn the piece of mango inside-out and cut away the cubed flesh from the skin. Place in a bowl, mash with a fork to a pulp, then add the cream and combine well. Spoon into a freezer container and freeze for about 1–1½ hours, until half frozen.

3 Meanwhile, put the apricots and orange juice in a small saucepan. Bring to a boil, then simmer gently until the apricots are soft, adding a little more juice if necessary, so that the apricots remain moist. Remove from the heat and set aside to cool.

4 Chop or dice the remaining mango as above and place in a bowl. Cut the papaya in half, remove the seeds and peel. Dice the flesh and add to the mango.

5 Pour the apricot sauce over the fruit and gently toss to coat all the fruit.

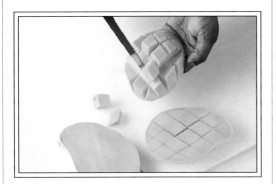

1 Take one thick slice from one of the mangoes and, while still on the skin, slash the flesh with a sharp knife in a criss-cross pattern to make cubes.

6 Stir the semi-frozen mango cream a few times until spoonable but not soft. Serve the fruit topped with the mango cream.

BANANA AND MELON IN ORANGE VANILLA SAUCE

M ost large supermarkets and health food stores sell vanilla beans. If vanilla beans are hard to find, use a few drops of natural vanilla extract instead.

INGREDIENTS
1 cup orange juice
1 vanilla bean or a few drops
vanilla extract
1 teaspoon grated orange rind
1 tablespoon sugar
4 bananas
1 honeydew melon
2 tablespoons lemon juice
shredded orange rind, to decorate

SERVES 4

1 Place the orange juice in a small saucepan with the vanilla bean, orange rind and sugar and gently bring to a boil.

2 Reduce the heat and simmer gently for 15 minutes or until the sauce is syrupy. Remove from the heat and allow to cool. If using vanilla extract, stir it into the sauce once it has cooled.

3 Coarsely chop the bananas and melon, place in a large serving bowl and toss with the lemon juice.

4 Pour the cooled sauce over the fruit and chill before serving, decorated with shreds of fresh orange rind.

BANANA MANDAZI

his is one of the most popular African desserts – simple to make and delicious to eat!

INGREDIENTS

1 egg
2 ripe bananas, coarsely chopped
²/₃ cup milk
¹/₂ teaspoon vanilla extract
2 cups self-rising flour
1 teaspoon baking powder
3 tablespoons sugar
vegetable oil, for deep frying
confectioners' sugar, to decorate

SERVES 4

1 Place the egg, bananas, milk, vanilla extract, flour, baking powder and sugar in a blender or food processor.

2 Process to make a smooth batter. It should have a creamy pourable consistency. If it is too thick, add a little extra milk. Set aside for 10 minutes.

3 Heat the oil in a heavy saucepan or deep fat fryer. When hot, carefully place spoonfuls of the mixture in the oil and fry, in batches, for 3–4 minutes, until golden.

4 Remove with a slotted spoon and drain on paper towels. Keep warm, then serve at once, sprinkled with confectioners' sugar.

TROPICAL FRUIT PANCAKES

ring a touch of tropical sunshine into your kitchen with these fruit-filled pancakes.

INGREDIENTS
1 cup self-rising flour
pinch of grated nutmeg
1 tablespoon sugar
1 egg
1¼ cups milk
1 tablespoon melted butter or margarine,
plus extra for frying
1 tablespoon fine dried
coconut (optional)
confectioners' sugar, to decorate
fresh cream, to serve

FOR THE FILLING
8 ounces ripe, firm mango
2 bananas
2 kiwi fruit
1 large orange
1 tablespoon lemon juice
2 tablespoons orange juice
1 tablespoon honey
2–3 tablespoons orange
liqueur (optional)

SERVES 4

1 Sift the flour, nutmeg and sugar into a large mixing bowl. In a separate bowl, beat the egg lightly, then beat in most of the milk. Add to the flour mixture and beat with a wooden spoon or whisk to make a thick, smooth batter.

2 Add the remaining milk, butter or margarine and coconut, if using, and continue beating until the batter is smooth and of a fairly thin, dropping consistency.

3 Melt a little butter in a large nonstick frying pan. Swirl to cover the pan, then pour in some batter to cover the bottom of the pan. Fry the pancake until golden brown, then toss or turn with a spatula. Repeat with the remaining mixture to make about eight pancakes in total.

4 Dice the mango, coarsely chop the bananas and slice the kiwi fruit. Cut away the peel and pith from the orange and cut into segments.

5 Place the fruit in a bowl. Mix the lemon and orange juices, honey and liqueur, if using, then pour over the fruit.

6 Spoon some fruit along the center of a pancake and fold over each side. Repeat with the others, then arrange on a plate, sprinkle with sugar and serve with cream.

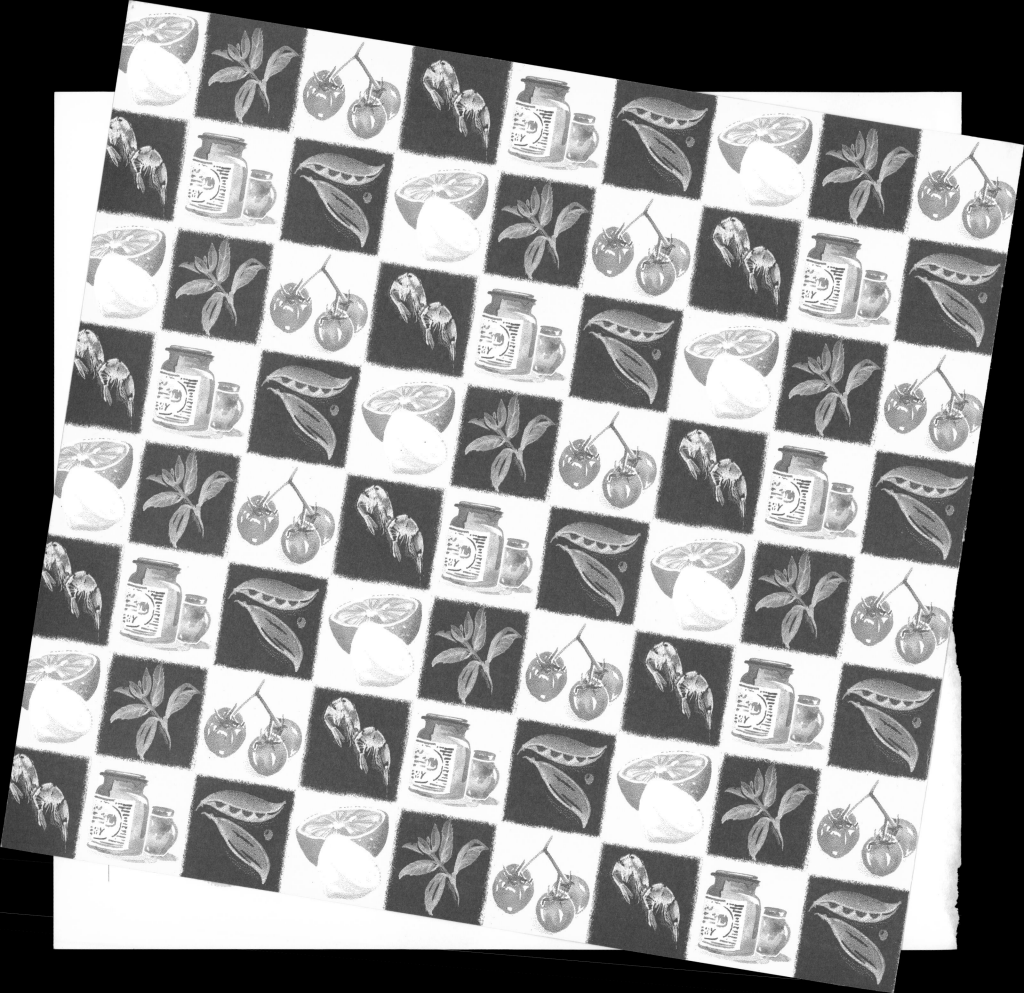